MW00414662

Enjoy Growing Your Own Great Rose Garden

A Definitive Rose Gardening Guide That Will Give You Superior Ideas On How To Grow Roses, Tips On Caring For Roses, Caring For Roses And A Lot More!

Carl P. Hawley

Disclaimer

This book is presented to you for informational purposes only and is not a substitution for any professional advice. The contents herein are based on the views and opinions of the author and all associated contributors.

While every effort has been made by the author and all associated contributors to present accurate and up to date information within this document, it is apparent technologies rapidly change. Therefore, the author and all associated contributors reserve the right to update the contents and information provided herein as these changes progress. The author and/or all associated contributors take no responsibility for any errors or omissions if such discrepancies exist within this document.

The author and all other contributors accept no responsibility for any consequential actions taken, whether monetary, legal, or otherwise, by any and all readers of the materials provided. It is the reader's sole responsibility to seek professional advice before taking any action on their part.

Readers results will vary based on their skill level and individual perception of the contents herein, and thus no guarantees, monetarily or otherwise, can be made accurately. Therefore, no guarantees are made.

Table of Contents

Introduction

Flowers are a great addition to any garden, and/or room's decor. The add color, fragrance, and elegance in what might be otherwise, dingy spaces. Nothing can offer quite as much as a great floral arrangement, especially if those flowers are roses.

Roses have always been a symbol of peace, love, friendship, and even death to all who see them. For centuries, roses have come to characterize great taste and eternity during events such as weddings, anniversaries, and birthdays. They are always the flower of choice when someone is hoping to create a bond with another.

Anyone can purchase roses in a gift shop or florist, but it takes a special person to want to grow their own roses. There are too many types of roses to list them all here, but this manual will be your comprehensive guide to planting and caring for your very own roses. By using this guide you will learn to:

· Plant your own roses

· Caring for your roses

· Pruning your roses properly

· Tips on arranging your rose bouquet

· Tips on drying roses

· How to use roses as gifts

· How to fertilize your roses

· How to water your roses properly

· How to prevent diseases in your roses

· How to treat diseases that your roses get infected with

· How to revive dead roses

· How to choose the best roses for your garden

That is a lot of stuff to learn by reading one simple manual, but this one has it all. By the time you have finished reading this, you will be prepared to add the beauty of roses to your garden.

Since roses are such a high maintenance flower, there is a great deal that you need to learn. At first glance, you may feel a bit overwhelmed by all of the things that you need to know before you can begin to plant them, but that will soon disappear after you read all of the easy to follow instructions mentioned in this guide.

Get ready to learn all you can about roses. This will be the best thing that you ever did for yourself and your family's garden.

Chapter 1 - Choosing the Right Rose for your Garden

There are literally hundreds of types of roses that you can grow in your garden. With such a selection to choose from, it can be extremely difficult to choose the rose that's right for you. To make this task a bit easier, I've added some crucial factors that you should consider, and some of the different types of roses to aid in your search.

· Color may seem like a trivial matter, but it is usually a factor to those that want to grow roses. Usually it is simply a matter of personal preference.

· The final growth height of a rose should be considered as it would be unattractive to grow roses that are higher than the area of the garden that it grows in. Some roses can grow to be as high as 20 feet.

· If you live in an area that is prone to cold winters, you would certainly want a rose that could survive during the off season.

· If certain fragrances invoke an allergic reaction, you would want to plant roses that have a softer fragrance than the others.

· You would certainly want to learn what the advantages and disadvantages would be if you were to choose certain roses over others.

· You will want to consider the size of your garden space, so that you can ensure proper exposure to the air and other elements as well.

· If you are hoping to make your roses into bouquets, you will want to know if they can be cut. Hybrid teas can. Some roses will fall apart at the petals if they are cut.

· You should also consider what other types of flowers or plants you intend on adding to the rose's environment. You want to add plants and flowers that will not create a damaging environment to your rose's ecosystem.

Some Common Types of Roses

After you get a sense of the type of roses that you would like to plant, you will naturally want to know which type of rose's best fit your ideas for planting. There are too many to list here, but I can list some of them for you. You should consult your nearest garden center for advice on whether your choice is fitting to your garden's abilities.

Landscape roses

Landscape roses are great for the novice gardener. They are disease resistant, and require a little bit less maintenance. Hybrid teas are not good for the novice.

Climbing Roses

These roses are different from the regular roses that are planted as they are trained to grow upward like vines. Most people like to use these for trellises, or buildings. Some of them are hybrid teas, wichuraine, and large flowered climbers. They are a beautiful addition to the look of one's house.

Shrub Roses

Shrub roses like the beautiful rugosa are both long blooming, and disease resistant. These are also great for the novice planter. They are gorgeous even when they are not in bloom because the foliage is so pretty.

Old Garden Roses

These roses are not very good for those with severe allergies to strong fragrances because they have a strong fragrant odor. However, they are disease resistant and continue to bloom for months at a time.

The Modern Rose

These are very special roses because they are the result of cross breeding the hybrid tea with the polyanthus. They are also referred to as Floribunda. They are a beautiful combination of the best those two flowers have to offer. They are long blooming, fragrant, and they are great for cutting.

Miniature Roses

Miniature roses are exactly what they sound like. They have all of the fragrance and beauty of a regular rose, but they have smaller blooms. These particular roses are great for indoor planting.

Chapter 2 - Planting Roses

The art of planting roses doesn't have to be a complicated thing to do. When you have the right knowledge there is no limit to how beautiful a garden or rosebush that you can create.

In this guide, you will not only have all of the right skills at your fingertips, but you will get 101 tips that you can use to grow your very own bed of roses. With this extensive manual at hand, you will never have to buy another bouquet again. Now you will have all of the beauty and delicious fragrance that roses can give you with you all the time.

Here are some of the best ideas and tips for planting your roses.

1.   Check with your local gardening center or florist for the best type of roses to grow in you climate. If you are a novice, you should look for disease resistant types of roses because they require a lot less maintenance.

2.   When planting roses, you want to pick a spot that is well lit in the morning. You also want an area that is sunlit for at least 6 hours a day. Roses need a great deal of light if they are to grow properly.

3. Pick an area that has plenty of well drained soil. Great soil has a PH level where the amount of acid in the soil is at about 5.5-7.0. You can get a testing kit for your soil at any garden center.

4. Organic matter like manure or lime helps to nourish the roots of your roses. You should soak the roots in water or puddle clay for many minutes, and cut off the root's ends that are broken.

5. The first 3-4 weeks after planting your roses, you should water them often. Usually this is when the top 2 inches of soil is dry. Roses need a lot of hydration and food to remain healthy.

6. Four weeks after planting, you should start soaking the bed every 2 weeks or so. You should do this in the morning for the best results.

7. Begin fertilization approximately 3 months after planting. Use 3-6 inches of mulch to control the moisture, temperature, and to stops weeds from coming up. Mulch also helps to lock in the vital nutrients your roses need in order to remain healthy.

8. Planting in the Spring is the best.

9. You want to plant your roses in an area that is well circulated with air. Your roses will not grow in an enclosed or tight area.

10. Dig a hole that is two times bigger than the amount of space that your roses take up. It makes it easier to plant them and creates a spaced area for them to grow with freedom. Poor circulation for your roses can cause fungal diseases. Using a larger hole also makes it easier for you to pull them up later and pot them if you'd like.

Watering Your Roses

Watering your roses can be a tricky thing. It is one of the most important aspects of taking care of your roses. Roses need almost as much water to stay healthy as people do. Of course there are quite a few things that must be considered before you water your roses. They are as follows:

· Like people, roses need more water during the hotter weather than during the colder ones. Heat makes the soil dry faster and the roses get "thirstier".

· Keep in mind that even during the rainier times, roses still need to be watered with fresh water because rain alone cannot provide the right amount of moisture for your roses.

· You want to water your roses in a manner that goes deep enough into the surrounding soil so that it reaches the roots. Try going approximately 45cm deep.

· You do not want to water the petals directly or the canes because it can cause fungal disease in your roses.

· To help you lower the risk of your roses getting diseases, mulch is a nice way to keep the soil moist, without allowing all of the fungal problems that too much moisture can cause.

· Watering your roses in the morning also helps to dry the dew off of the leaves.

· Once your roses are fully established, you should water them once a week. You should do it twice a week if its in the hotter months.

Chapter 3 - Fertilizing Your Roses

It is really important to fertilize your roses. That is how your roses get their much needed nutrients. Roses are much like people in the things that they need in order to remain healthy. Just like people they need water and food (fertilizer).

Most types of roses have to be fertilized frequently to keep them growing at a fast pace. You should fertilize with a fertilizer that is slow to release like fish emulsion or Osmocote at planting time. Be certain to follow the instructions properly from the label.

Avoid over fertilizing during the winter because by trying to promote new growth in the winter will make your roses more available to freeze damage.

Important Tip: You should never fertilize plants that are heat or water stressed. Water stressed plants that grow under a lot of heat will cause leaf and bud burn.

You want a steady temperature of approximately 70-80 degrees because your plants will get the most nutrients that are available to the plants. During the growing season, you can give the plants a water soluble fertilizer every two weeks.

Chapter 4 - Caring for Your Roses

Taking proper care of your roses can seem like a very taxing, and time consuming thing to do, but the results of such care far more than make up for it.

Unfortunately, roses are the most difficult flower to manage and keep healthy; however, all good things require high maintenance.

There are many small things that have to be done to keep your roses looking their best, but all of those small things add up to one very large one. Here are some great tips for the regular upkeep of your roses.

1. You should prune your roses in the early spring. Or at least once the others start budding because the buds will eventually become new branches later.

2. You should cut the dead and damaged branches first. Next, you should cut all but five of the leftover healthy branches. They should end up at about the thickness of a pencil.

3. Cut the bushes by approximately one third or one half, depending on how tall you want them. Cutting above the outward facing buds, Which is the buds that is on the outside of the rose bush because this

will help the bud to grow upward; which will make the center of the bud open up for better air circulation and shape.

4. You should always sharpen your hand shears before pruning, and prune the climbing roses with caution. The branches have a tendency to overlap and you wouldn't want to prune the wrong branches.

5. Mulching is necessary because it helps to keep your maintenance down a bit. Mulching requires your roses to need a lot less watering, weeding and helps prevent diseases. The best mulches are organic ones like wood chips, pine needles, and grass clippings.

6. Protect your roses during the winter months by adding a few extra inches of soil to the base of your roses. This should provide the extra needed heat in the winter.

7. You should avoid the white plastic cones when doing your winter protection because they trap too much heat during the winter thaw. They are also quite unattractive.

8. You should feed your roses water often, but lightly. When you water your roses, avoid directly watering the foliage because it will cause fungal diseases. You should water the roses at the roots.

9. Keep the area around your roses cleared to prevent them from getting locked in an area that doesn't provide enough circulation.

Chapter 5 - Pruning Your Roses

Pruning your roses is one of the most needed and the most annoyingly difficult tasks that goes with proper rose care. It takes a steady hand the proper procedure to ensure the best possible roses that you can get.

Pruning your roses is basically the act of getting rid of dead and damaged pieces, and teaching the new growth to grow in the correct outward facing direction. That just means that you are training them to grow facing the outside of the shrub or bush. This gives your roses the correct amount of circulating air to thrive in.

Here is a list of the proper techniques to guide through the pruning process.

· Soak your pruning shears in equal parts of water and bleach. This will help to protect your roses from diseases and insects.

· Pruning in the early spring, just after the snow melts is best. However you want to do it before any new growth appears. The best time would be when the buds are swelled, or red.

· Hand shears are the best tool for pruning the smaller branches. (about 4 ½ inches thick) Loppers are best for the branches that are thicker or the thickness of a pencil. This will make it easier. You should use a heavy pair of rose gloves to avoid the thorns.

· You want to get rid of the winter protection that you set up like cones, burlap, and mounded soil.

· You want to get rid of the dead wood first. (That would be the black wood that is black inside as well as out).

· Next, you wan to get rid of the thinner wood, which is the stems that are thinner than a pencil.

· Cut all of the branches that cross or overlap one another because these are often diseased or will become so.

· Keep the remaining five healthy branches. These are often dark green. You will want to make your roses fluted or vases shaped, with an open center, and keep them from touching or overlapping each other.

· Cut your healthy canes to be about one to four feet long, or whatever size that you prefer.

· Cut you roses properly so that they stay healthy. Cut so that the bud is facing outside of the bush and at a 45 degree angle that slopes inward so that you can keep promoting the outward growth.

· You should use bypass pruners that work like scissors and not the anvil types because the anvils crush the stems and make the roses more available to diseases.

Chapter 6 - Planting Potted Roses

 It is common for people that have received roses in pots as gifts to fall so in love with their roses that they may want to replant them in their own garden. Adding a rose bush to any garden can be the best choice that you ever made.

 Planting potted roses doesn't have to be a taxing experience. With the right knowledge given to you in simple step by step format can make the task a great deal of fun. Here are all of the steps that you will need in order to plant your potted roses.

· You should plant contained roses in the spring, after you are absolutely positive that there is no chance for a return of the frost. If you live in a warmer climate like Florida or California, you will want to plant in the early autumn, once the weather has cooled off a bit.

· You will want to choose roses that do not have any flowers on them because you are simply trying to establish your roses. You are not trying to make your roses flower just yet. If you have to, trim the flowers off of them before you plant them.

· You definitely want to choose the right environment for your roses. You will want to plant them in an area of the garden that is susceptible to a lot of light in the morning, (at least 6 hours worth) because early morning light helps to dry the dew off of the flowers, which will help prevent fungal diseases.

· If you want the transition of your roses from a pot to your garden to go smoothly, you will need to prepare your soil very well. You want your soil to be well drained for the health of your roses.

· Once you have prepared your soil, you will want to work several spadesful of composte into the planting hole after digging in a hole that is about two feet deep.

· Tap your rose from its original container and plant it. You will also want to position it so that the soil level of the rose matches the soil level of the surrounding soil.

· Lastly, you will want to dig a mote-like ring around the rose so that you can pool the water.

That's all there is to planting potted roses. See that was not so difficult was it? As you probably noticed, it is a lot like planting your roses that were never potted, but of course with some slight differences. It can be a very rewarding thing, to plant your very own rose garden.

Chapter 7- Growing Organic Roses

Many people are now getting into growing all things organic. Farmers are doing it with produce and meats, so it is natural that you might want to grow your roses that way also. Many people have problems using the pesticides and insecticides that go along with growing roses and keeping them healthy. Well now you can use more natural methods of growing your roses. This section will show you how in a step by step method.

1.   Each bush that you want to plant will need to have a foot of space all around it so that the flowers can get the proper amount of circulation. It also helps to prevent leaf diseases for your roses.

2.   You will want to purchase organic roses. You will want to buy roses that have a sturdy green stem and no blemishes on them. Bare root roses are best for this.

3.   Along with roses that have green stems, you will need to look for stems that have evenly spaced leaves that are close together.

4.   You will need to use well drained soil so that you can promote the healthy growth that will give the

flower all of the water and nutrients that it needs from the root to the flower's head.

5.   Fix the soil so that you can build organically. You should use a raised bead if drainage is a constant problem. Ask your local garden center rep about how best to fix your soil to be organically correct.

6.   Soak your bare root roses in a large container of composte tea for many hours before you plant them.

7.   You must mound up enough good organic sol that is mixed with an equal amount of composte in the middle so that you can spread the roots out and down from where they meet at the trunk.

8.   Now, plant the rose at the point where the stem breaks into the root so that it is at soil level, or approximately 1 inch below the top level if you live in an area that is prone to hard winters

9.   You have to check your bare root roses first. If your roots grow out in a tight circle, you have to cut a straight slice down each of its four sides. A knife is good for this. Then you will dig a hole that is 2 inches deeper than the container and at least twice as wide.

10. Mix your organic soil garden soil with an equal amount of composte and use your hands to gently spread the roots into the soil mix.

11. You have to mulch to help you prevent your roses from being exposed to weeds, and water stress complications. It will also ensure that your roses remain at their lowest possible maintenance level.

12. You must feed your roses organically also. Fertilize with organic fertilizer and maintain a regular watering schedule.

13. Water your organic roses deep at the planting, and then once every week after that during growing season so that you can promote deep roots. Watering in the early morning is best.

14. You must cultivate the top inch of your soil around each of your roses and fertilize on a monthly basis with a balanced organic fertilizer. You will need a good granular type of fertilizer that you can work into the soil. Either that, or you can use a fish emulsion or seaweed based product that you can mix with water because it has all of the necessary nutrients that a healthy flower needs. Check the ingredients listed on the labels to ensure that they have nitrogen, phosphorus, potassium, iron and calcium.

15. To help protect your bed against the various types of pests and insects that can plague your roses, put sticky yellow bars every ten feet to catch them.

16. You may use an organic pesticide if the problem is bad.

17. If your pest problem is severe enough, you may use insecticidal soap to spray over your roses.

Now you have all of the necessary knowledge that you need to grow your own bed of earth friendly roses. Your flowers will be just as beautiful as those that are not grown organically, and will likely have the healthiest life span that a rose can get.

Organic roses have some of the best color and "immune systems" that a rose can have. The fragrance of them can't be beaten. Of course, it still helps to know how to prevent your roses from being taken over by diseases. The next section will help you with that.

Chapter 8 - Preventing Common Rose Diseases

Just like people, roses are susceptible to diseases and various other health problems. Many of the problems that come with having roses are relatively easy to take care of, but it is always better to stop them all together rather than having to cure them later. Here are some of the ways that you can prevent diseases from reaching your roses.

1. The easiest way to prevent diseases from inhabiting your roses is to buy roses that are low maintenance like shrubs and landscape roses.

2. Planting your roses properly in areas that have a lot of sun (at least 6 hours in the morning), air circulation and good compost for faster draining can prevent many problems later.

3. Keeping different types of flowers and plants in with your roses will help to provide your roses with a better and more balanced ecosystem to live in.

4. Fertilize your plants in the proper manner. Roses need their food too! (see section on fertilizing for the best methods)

5. Watering your roses correctly and in the morning is a good way to keep fungal diseases from hitting your roses. (see section on watering for the best techniques)

6. A two inch layer of mulch at the base of your roses is a good way to keep soil born diseases at bay.

Fixing Diseased and Problem Roses

It seems that even with the best of prevention techniques and caring for your roses, you cannot always stop diseases and problems from affecting your roses. For all of the problems your roses can encounter, there are just as many ways to fix them. All it takes is a little bit of tender loving care, and the right techniques. Here are some of those techniques to help your roses look their best.

Aphids and Spider Mites

Aphids are a greenish brown insect that suck the juices from roses, and can eventually cause your roses to dry out. To effectively treat them, simply blast your roses with soapy water.

Black Spots

Black spots are a fungal disease that causes the canes to turn black or brown in spots on the foliage. To remedy this, simply prune the affected areas and throw out the clippings. Do not water the head to prevent this from happening again.

Canker

A canker is another fungal disease that causes the canes to turn black or brown. All you have to do is prune the canes just below the canker in the early spring.

Midge

A midge is a tiny maggot that causes the rose's buds to blacken from the damage. If you want to fix this problem, prune the affected area and then destroy it.

Rust

Rust is a disease that creates an orange powder in the center of the rose. It is caused by wet and calm winter weather. Putting in some spider mites can help with this because they hate the water. You should consult your local garden center about the best insecticide to use in order to get rid of the spider mites. Once you have chosen the insecticide, spray every 7-10 days until it is under control.

Powder Mildew

You can put an end to powder mildew by making a mixture of 1 gallon of water

2 TBSP of baking soda

1 TBSP of Murphy's Oil Soap

Spray over the roses in the morning every two weeks until the overall temperature around the roses reaches 80 degrees.

Chapter 9 - Give Your Roses a Springtime Boost

Every spring people get a boost of energy. It is like the very air in the spring time is rejuvenating in itself. Natural passions and new loves are often born in the spring, and old loves get a nice spark between them. Spring is definitely the best time of year.

The same goes for roses. It is in the spring that people begin planting or replenishing their rose gardens. For those bushes that are already established, spring is the time to see new buds and blooms trying to be born.

If you are interested in helping your roses get an even bigger boost in the spring, you may want to try this special tonic that is used to give your roses a strong boost of all of the nutrients that your roses need in order for them to grow strong, healthy and produce a lot of buds. Try this recipe for the greatest spring start to your roses.

1. Be certain to apply in the early spring after you have removed any of the necessary winter protection that you put up.

Here is a list of the ingredients that you will need to make this mixture. You should mix them in a 5 gallon tub or bucket.

· 2 cups of alfalfa meal

· 2 cups of Epsom salt

· 2 cups of fish meal

· 2 cups of gypsum

· 2 cups of greensand

· 1 cup of bone meal

2. You will first have to pull back the mulch that has been placed around your rose bush.

3. You will next, want to work one cup of this tonic into the top inch of soil if you have a smaller bush.

4. You will do best to use a trowel or a hand cultivator for larger bushes. (that would be bushes that are 6 feet or taller) For these sizes, you will need to use three or four cups.

5. Now you will have to replace the mulch and water your roses very well.

Tip #1: You can do this again in the middle of June if you want to keep your roses blooming. Just scratch 2 cups of the mixture into the soil.

Tip #2: You should wear a dust mask while you are mixing your ingredients for the tonic.

Chapter 10 - Drying Your Roses

There are many reasons why you might want to dry your roses. Some people just want to keep a memento of a special moment. Perhaps they are a part of a wedding that you went to; maybe they were a gift from a mate, friend, or family member. Whatever your reasons for doing it, this is the section where you will learn to dry your roses properly.

There two ways that you can dry your roses that are a cheap and relatively easy.

Air Drying

Air drying is by far the easiest and cheapest method of drying flowers including roses. It is simple; all you have to do is follow these simple instructions.

Start with perfect and unflawed roses on their stems. If the roses are not in perfect condition, they will wither and the petals will fall off.

1. Remove any leaves that may be on the branches.

2. Bunch them up together in a manner that lets them fan out.

3. Tie the bottom with string or a rubber band.

4. Hang them upside down in a dark, dry place for two to three weeks to be certain that they are completely dry.

Sand Drying

1. Start by picking the roses that are in perfect condition. They shouldn't have any dew on them and the stems should be dry as well.

2. You can reinforce the stems and blossom with either white glue or florist wire.

3. For florist wire, you will want to cut off most of the stem. Leave about one inch of stem.

4. Push about 3 inches of wire through the stem and right through the flower head.

5. Next, you want to bend the end of the wire into a hook over each rose head and pull it down. This helps to keep the head secured to the stem.

6. When choosing to use the glue, begin by diluting the glue in a dab of water.

7. You will take a toothpick and dab a thin coat of the glue mixture at the base of each petal.

8. Next, you will work the glue into the base of the stems of each flower so that you can attach each petal to the base, wait till the glue dries completely

9. Now for the sand, slowly and carefully cover the flowers with sand in deep open boxes.

10. Make the sand in the box deep enough to hold the flowers upright.

11. Sit each flower in the sand filled box and slowly pour sand around the base, around the sides, and over and under the petals. You should pour the sand evenly so that you can preserve the flowers natural shape.

12. You will want to wait for the flowers to dry while facing upright.

13. Put the boxes with the roses in a dry space that is warm and brightly lit. This will ensure that your roses will maintain their bright color.

14. Let them dry for one to three weeks.

15. If you want more muted colors, you will want to dry them in a more humid area.

16. To remove the sand, tip the drying container slightly so that the sand can fall off the flowers.

17. Remove each flower one by one.

Now you have successfully learned how to dry your roses so that they are ready for you to do whatever you'd like with them. These dried flowers will make great decorations for any room in your house or office, or whatever else you'd like to do.

Chapter 11 - Cold Climate Roses

Most roses will grow just about anywhere, and in any type of climate. Certain roses do not function very well in cold climates, but will grow just as well in any other. Hybrid Teas are not however, a cold climate rose. They must be grown in a warmer climate like Florida. They simply don't have the necessary winter protection that some cold climate flowers have.

If you live in an area that is prone to harsh winters, you will likely find it relatively easy to find good, cold climate roses at your local garden center. It is necessary to plant cold climate roses in areas that are prone to winters because planting anything else would be a waste of your time as they couldn't survive properly during the winter frost.

Cold climate roses are great for many reasons. They are very low maintenance flowers, especially good for the novice. Cold climate roses also have their very own protection set up against diseases and bacteria that can plague any flower. Here a brief list of cold climate roses. Naturally, there are many more, but to list them all would make up the entirety of this guide.

The cold climate roses are as follows:

· Rugosas

· Griffith Buck

· Modern Roses

· Centrifolias

· Species Roses

· Gallica

· Alba

· Shrub Roses

These are just some of the cold climate roses that will thrive during the harsh winters of some localities. If you live in an area that is prone to harsh winters, you may want to see if your local garden center has any of these to start with.

Chapter 12 - Revive Wilting Roses

With all of the possible diseases that a rose can pick up, you would think that anybody would be crazy to even plant them. They are such high maintenance flowers that it would seem to some to be far too much work just to have a bit of beauty in your garden.

As this guide has already stated, there are a great deal of things that can be done to help prevent diseases and pests from damaging your roses. It all seems like so much to do for flowers that only have a life span of about 6-10 days. Of course a healthy bed of roses will constantly produce new buds so that you will rarely even notice anyway.

There is also the problem of wilting and drooping roses once they are placed in vases when they are given as gifts. Roses look so beautiful in any room that they sit in. They add an elegance that is unsurpassed by any other flower.

As beautiful as roses are, they do have a certain vulnerability that is common for every flower. They are prone to sag, droop and wilt after a few days exposure to a vase. Anybody would like to preserve that beauty for as long as possible and think that its hopeless, but I will show you how you can save your roses if this happens to you.

1. Take your roses from the vase.

2. Separate the roses, but keep them emerged in Luke warm water as you do it.

3. Make a fresh cut on the stem, again while it remains in the water because you don't want to get air into the stem.

4. Take each flower, one by one and roll them in newspaper and close the paper with a rubber band to keep it from unrolling.

5. Put each rose while still wrapped in the newspaper in a sink or tub filled with water and let them soak for several hours while still separate.

6. Once they have soaked, unwrap them carefully, and place them in a vase of fresh warm water.

7. If you want to preserve the health of your roses, put some 7up in the water to help prevent any bacteria that can clog up the stem.

Extra tip: Roses droop for one of two reasons. Either they had been cut too early when put into the vase, or they may have been out of water too long before putting them into the vase.

Chapter 13 - Roses as Gifts

 Roses are a perfect choice as a gift because they go with any occasion or special moment that you want to share with someone special to you. Using roses as gifts is especially common during Valentine's Day, but sometimes, there are other reasons to give a special gift.

 The best part about roses, is that they are perfect to express almost anything that you want to say without you having to say a word. If you went out on a date and want to convey that you wish to remain friends only, sending a small bouquet of roses that are yellow or pink is the nicest way to do it.

 Here are a few of the occasions where roses are not only a perfect gift, but that will let whomever you are giving the gift know exactly how you feel.

· Anniversaries

· Birthdays

· Graduations

· House Warming

· Getting a new job

· Getting a promotion

· And various other holidays

Now that you know what some of the occasions that make roses a very special addition. You may want to know how you can put them together in different ways that can be different and original. Here is a nice list of the different ways that roses can be turned into gifts that will always be remembered.

Bouquets

This is the most commonly used method of giving roses as a gift. Rose bouquets look great in any color when they are mixed with Spanish moss and an occasional green leaf plant. It is an attractive and simple gift that goes with any occasion.

Potpourri

Potpourri is a lovely and simple way to get all of the great joys out of a rose, without having to do all of the upkeep that goes along with giving fresh roses. Turning roses into potpourri is a simple and rewarding process that gives off a delicious fragrance that lasts for weeks.

All you have to do is follow the air dry technique that is listed in this manual. Once the roses are dried, simply take the blooms and separate them. You can put the shreds in a nice porcelain container, or a sealed piece of hosiery.

Dried Bouquets

Dried rose bouquets are beautiful and last as long as you want them to. All you have to do for this is to follow the sanding method for drying your roses, and plant them in a makeshift pot. You can mix your roses with dried green, fresh or fake moss and any other dried flower that you would like to use in your arrangement. It is an economical and fragrant gift to give anyone. You can also ask your local garden center professional which types of clear sprays you can use to give your flowers a glossy look.

Candied Roses

You do not necessarily have to use completely fresh or dried roses alone in making up the perfect gift. You can mix real roses with candied or chocolate roses to add to the originality of your gift. It is a delicious way to let someone know that you care about them.

Summary

By now, you have learned all the things that you need to know in order to grow the perfect arrangement of roses. You have learned how to:

· Plant and grow your own flowers

· How to help keep your roses disease and problem free

· How to grow roses organically

· The best types of cold climate roses

· How to dry your roses

· How to use roses as great gift ideas

You have naturally learned all there is to know about roses. By now, you should be ready to go out into your garden and begin preparing your soil for their lovely addition.

Although there wasn't a special section about mulching your roses, the process was mentioned many times during this guide to roses. There really isn't much to say about mulch other than to point out that when you do lay down mulch in your garden, you should be sure to enclose the area around it to prevent spillage.

There are many ways that you can make a nice looking enclosure for your mulched area. Your local garden center can show you the traditional rubber enclosure that resembles a small black or brown gate that sits about two to three inches above the ground. This type of enclosure will not hinder the air supply to your roses, but it looks very attractive.

Another type of enclosure that you can use for your mulched area is made out of wood. You can choose from many different stains and it is easy to install. All you will really need is a hammer that works well. Again you will not want to make it too high so as not to hinder the air circulation to your roses.

Finally, you can also choose to use any number of designer plastic mini gates. Some are plain picket fences; some are designed to look like flowers or cars. It is really cool for those of you that like to add a little spice to the look of your garden.

I don't want this manual to discuss mulching too much, I just wanted to make sure that you closed this book with enough knowledge to know that you will never need another book again because you have all that you need right here.

32727003R00029

Made in the USA
Lexington, KY
01 June 2014